...and he shall appear as an
ANGEL OF LIGHT

✝

MARY E. PRESTON

iUniverse, Inc.
Bloomington

...and he shall appear as an ANGEL OF LIGHT

All Scripture quotations, unless otherwise indicated, are from
the King James Version of the Bible (public domain).

Scripture quotations marked (NKJV) are taken from the New King James Version.
Copyright 1982 by Thomas Nelson, Inc. Used by permission. All rights reserved.

Scripture quotations marked (NLT) are taken from the *Holy Bible, New
Living Translation.* Copyright 1996. Used by permission of Tyndale
House Publishers, Inc., Wheaton, IL 60189 USA. All rights reserved.

iUniverse books may be ordered through booksellers or by contacting:

iUniverse
1663 Liberty Drive
Bloomington, IN 47403
www.iuniverse.com
1-800-Authors (1-800-288-4677)

ISBN: 978-1-4697-9631-4 (sc)
ISBN: 978-1-4697-9632-1 (e)

Printed in the United States of America

iUniverse rev. date: 4/12/2012

I am dedicating this book to a man named Larry. He was in a Christian bookstore where my husband and I were browsing, and we began a conversation with him about the return of Jesus Christ. Much to my surprise, he was so confused about the second coming of Christ that I was heartsick. I told my husband, "I can't stand by any longer while people remain ignorant about Christ's return."

Since my conversation with Larry, I have had an overwhelming desire to come forward and share what I learned many years ago about Christ's return.

I hope you find this book at your nearest bookstore or online, and when you read it, Larry, God's love and grace will not only inform you but also transform your life—as well as the lives of others.

Contents

Scripture References

Angel of Light – 2 Corinthians 11:14

Apollyon-Abaddon – Revelation 9–11

Lucifer–Son of the Morning – Isaiah 14:12

Son of Perdition – John 17–12

War in Heaven – Revelation 12:4

Satan's Wisdom – Ezekiel 28:3

Satan – A Wolf in Sheep's Clothing – Matthew 7:15

Satan – Walking as a Roaring Lion – 1 Peter 5:8

False Christs – Matthew 24:24

Bodies Changed – 1 Corinthians 15:52

Holy Spirit Speaks – Luke 21:14–15

Milk of Word – 1 Peter 2:2

Buy or Sell – Revelation 13:17

Peace, Peace – Not War – Revelation 13:4

The Scorpion – Revelation 9:3, 10–11

Interpretation of Rapture – Matthew 24:40–42

Time Shortened – Mark 13:20

Ten Virgins – Matthew 25:1–12

Thirsting – Psalm 42:1–2

Willful King – Daniel 11:36

Early Church Suffers and Believe They Are in "the Tribulation" – 2 Thessalonians 1:4–5

Man of Sin – 2 Thessalonians 2:1–4

Covering Cherub – Ezekiel 28:14

Satan in Garden – Genesis 3:13

Satan Tempts Christ – Matthew 4:3–9

Strong Delusion – 2 Thessalonians 2:11–12

Great Tribulation – Matthew 24:21–24

Christian Persecution – Mark 13:9–12

Satan Called Death – Hebrews 2:14

Meat of Word – Hebrews 5:14

Seven Last Plagues – Revelation 16:1–17

Hiding Place – Isaiah 33:15–16, Psalm 32:7, Psalm 119:114

Paul's Work – Philippians 2:16–17

Last Trump – 1 Corinthians 15:52

Sound Doctrine – 2 Timothy 4:3–4

Hireling – John 10:12–13

Fire from Heaven – Revelation 13:13

If Possible, Elect Deceived – Matthew 24:24

End-Time Generation – Matthew 24:34

Armies Gather against Jerusalem – Zechariah 14:1–3

Rocks to Fall on Them – Revelation 6:16

Desolation Is Nigh – Luke 21:20

God Is for Us, Who Can Be against Us? – Romans 8:31

Never Leave or Forsake Us – Hebrews 13:5

God Is a Jealous God – Exodus 34:13–17

Strong's Concordance of the King James Bible — In the Greek New Testament

ANTI – Greek #473 – Means instead of or substitution.

Antichrist – Greek #500 – Means opponent of the Messiah.

Spurious messiah – Greek #5580 – Means pseudo, or false, Christ and refers back to Greek #5547 and #5571. The Greek numbers 5547, 5571, and 5580 are all tied together in referring to the antichrist.

Spurious prophet – Greek #5578 – Means a pretend foreteller or religious imposter.

Preface

One morning in the mid 1990s, I awakened around 5:00 a.m., feeling as though I should get up and pray. I always set a time in the morning to pray and have my morning devotional, but it wasn't at 5:00 a.m. I was willing to get up and pray, and I did so for several weeks, but then I became restless, wondering why I was to rise so early. I began to feel confused as to what God was doing and where He was leading me because I didn't see or feel any real guidance in my life, other than my being obedient and getting up at exactly 5:00 a.m.

On one of these early mornings, after I had had my early morning devotional, I asked God, "What is it that You would have me do?" It was still early in the morning, so I could either sit there or go back to bed. I was very tempted to do the latter, as I was not a morning person. I wasn't sure what to do, so I turned on the television and began channel surfing. I stopped on a channel where a minister was preaching on the Antichrist and the end times; his program started at 5:00 a.m.

For years, I had been interested in end-time prophecy, so I turned on the TV every morning to listen. I kept up with his scriptures in my KJV (King James Version) of the Bible and wrote down as many as I could keep up with. I ordered myself a *Strong's Concordance* of the KJV Bible and began to study. I studied everything I could find on the Antichrist, and it all started to make sense. It felt like a breath of fresh air coming through a window, eliminating all the confusion I had been taught in my earlier years.

I had always been under the impression that the Antichrist would come out of the Mideast or that he would be a pope in the last days. I do believe many pastors (perhaps ignorantly) mislead their congregations about what will happen at the "end of time."

I was so excited about this new discovery that I began telling my family. Some believed, and some scoffed, but I continued to inform them anyway. I must admit, I was very disappointed that I couldn't persuade them, even with all the Scripture I had presented. I told myself, "At least they have heard, and when these things begin to happen, surely they will know it to be true."

I've asked them as I am asking you: if it doesn't click with you and the Holy Spirit hasn't touched your heart right now, put it on the shelf. It is my prayer that it will be revealed to you in God's own timing.

What we believe about the end times is so important because it can mean the difference between life and death: whom will we serve? I will explain more on this later.

I have no degrees or doctorates in theology, so I can understand why people will question my ability to write a book on such a controversial subject. Nevertheless, I have been an avid student of "end-times prophecy" for over sixteen years, and my sources for writing this book are the King James Bible and *Strong's Concordance*. I wanted to know who the "Antichrist" was, and I discovered this by researching the topic in the Bible, using my concordance as my guide. I was also influenced by the minister whom I watched on television at 5:00 a.m., who came across with a no-sugar-coating, "tell it like it is" approach as he presented end-times prophecy while using only the Word of God and *Strong's Concordance*. God has definitely impressed upon my heart to write what has been revealed to me through His Word. This is a documentary using Scripture (not a sermon) of how most of the world will be misled at the end of time.

I am going to write what I have learned in a very simple dialogue so that there will be minimal confusion in presenting these biblical facts. Many times we take the simple things in God's Word and make them hard to understand, but God takes the hard things and makes them so very simple. Ask God for eyes to see and ears to hear. God uses the weak to confound the wisdom of the wise (see 1 Corinthians 1:27).

If you receive this information and are touched by the Holy Spirit, you too will want to share it with everyone you know.

Let's Get Started

Get yourself a King James Version of the Bible and a *Strong's Concordance* of the Bible (not a *Young's Concordance*), and let's see what we can discover. In case you don't wish to invest in a *Strong's Concordance*, I will note the references for you, or maybe you can borrow the book from your pastor or a library.

As long as I do not take verses out of context or add to or take away from what Scripture says, I know the Holy Spirit will be with me and guide me with what I am about to share. There are those who will say this is exactly what I am doing—that I am confused and mistaken about these Scriptures—but that's all right, because it will tell me they have at least read the book, and when they see these things happening upon the earth, my hope is that they will recall what they read months or years ago, and it will all fit together and have meaning.

What I am about to share with all of you is really so simple that a fifth-grade student could understand with the proper documentation. Unfortunately, it may be too simple for some. Why? Because we must come to Christ with the mind of a child: eager to learn, nonjudgmental, and not so steeped in tradition that our spiritual eyes and ears are closed.

"What do you mean by that?" you ask. A good example would be the belief that what your great, great grandpa and sweet Aunt Mary believed a hundred years ago was good enough for them and so is still good enough for you. This is what I am talking about: your spiritual eyes and ears are closed. What they believed a hundred years ago or even twenty years ago does not pertain to you in the end times. Am I saying that we should disregard sound doctrine from the church that has been handed down to us for hundreds of years? God forbid! But Revelation is for the future. Even Daniel was told to seal up the book until the end of time; it was not for his generation. I think we can all agree that we are now living in the end times, and what we need to know now is not exactly the same as what our forefathers were taught or had to be concerned with.

Are We Living in the End Times?

Point #1: "And when ye shall see *Jerusalem compassed with armies,* then know that the desolation thereof is nigh" (See Luke 21:20, KJV). This quote is "end times prophecy." We will learn later what the desolation or desolator is that the Bible is talking about and how we are to react.

Note: Israel was established as a nation in 1948, and God declared this time to be a benchmark regarding his return. The Lord spoke in (Matthew 24:34) that this generation (meaning the generation at the end of time) would not pass away until all these things prophesied would be fulfilled. Most Bible scholars agree that a generation is seventy to eighty years. If you add this onto the time when Israel was declared a nation in 1948, you can see the time is near—possibly at the door.

We are not to set an exact time for Christ's return, but God does give us certain occurrences that will be happening close to the end of time, and we are to look up and know that his time is near. We will discuss many of these signs in the chapters to come. When we see armies surrounding Israel, ready to annihilate them—"look up, for your salvation is near" (Luke 21:28, NLT; see also Zechariah 14:1–3). I will discuss this further on, and you will understand why God allows the destruction in Zechariah 14 to occur.

Point #2: The Condition of Man. I am going to quote an article by the Associated Press concerning mixing human and animal DNA.

(*Red Orbit*, November 10, 2009, Study to Focus on Mixing Human and Animal DNA, taken from the Internet on Google http://www. redorbit.com/news/science/1783808/study.)

> For some time researchers have been replacing animal genes with human genes or growing human organs in animals.
>
> Meanwhile, the regulation on how much human DNA can be put into an animal is vague, and scientists are now trying to determine where the line should be drawn on experiments that use human material in animals.
>
> "Do these constructs challenge our idea of what it is to be human?" said Bobrow, a professor of medical genetics at Cambridge University.
>
> "It is important that we consider these questions now so that appropriate boundaries are recognized and research is able to fulfill its potential."

If you would like to read the article in its entirety, you can Google "Mixing Human and Animal DNA. http://www.redorbit.com/news/ science/1783808/study." It seems that man is not content with being the one created by God and honoring the Creator. Rather, he wants to become a Creator himself. In the latter days, "Knowledge shall be increased" (see Daniel 12:4), and "men shall be lovers of their own selves ... more than lovers of God" (see 2 Timothy 3:2–4).

These experiments have been going on for some time now, but how much further these scientists are going to take this remains to be seen. I would imagine they are determined to do anything they can get away with. Everything starts out so innocently, such as wanting to find a cure for a particular disease or malady. Later, however, these experiments turn into something diabolical.

God does things in a natural way. Nature, if not disturbed, produces kind after kind. If you cross a donkey and a horse, you get a mule, but the mule cannot reproduce; it is sterile. Is crossing a horse with a donkey evil? No, because they are still in the same category as mammals, and there was not any involvement with laboratory experiments. But now, possibly, there will be experimental mixing of animal and human DNA in a diabolical way that will create some mutant form of animal/human—real science fiction stuff! Only it may not be so fictional after all.

I know these experiments aren't starting out diabolically, but what happens if they get out of control? Humans, without God in their lives and equipped with advanced science and experimentation such as DNA mixing, can and will go beyond certain boundaries. What's to stop them from trying to produce a superhuman race? Hitler would have loved this.

Point #3: *Be watchful.* If Christians would take a moment and look around, they would see a religious power becoming more numerous right here in the United States. This religious belief needs to be brought to the attention of every Christian.

Let me direct your attention to "Jesus Will Return," by Harun Yahya. This is presented in a question-and-answer format. I believe it is a real eye-opener if you will read the article in its entirety. Here is an excerpt:

Question: "What kind of relationship will there be between the Prophet Jesus and the Mahdi when both are on the earth?"

Answer: "According to the hadiths, when the Prophet Jesus returns to earth he will act together with the Mahdi, and the two will combine all their powers to bring religious moral values to prevail in the world. The Prophet Jesus will eliminate the Anti-Christ (Dajjal), the leader of the atheistic system in the world and the Mahdi will assist him in that struggle. The Prophet Jesus and the Mahdi are two brothers with great love for one another in this world and in the hereafter. They will share the same thoughts and beliefs. The Mahdi will be the spiritual leader of the Islamic world, and the Prophet Jesus that of the Christian world. Under their twin leadership the world will enjoy great peace, security and happiness. In my view, the Prophet Jesus has also returned to earth, but he too is hidden. He is obliged to conceal himself because of the terrorist and political attacks he would be exposed to. However, he too will emerge in the very near future and together with the Mahdi will embark upon his intellectual struggle." (You can visit his website, www.jesuswill return.com.)

Unless Christians are totally asleep or in a coma, I do not see how they can miss what is beginning to happen: a one-world religion and government are about to be set up! I always wondered how the whole world would worship an Antichrist (instead of Christ) while there are so many divisive religious beliefs. I can now understand how it is possibly coming together.

Hopefully, you can understand my urgency in writing this book on the end times and why we must study and be aware of events going on about us so that we will not be lured into a slumberous state of mind. Let us become students of God's Word, filled with excitement and curiosity! Read up on current events pertaining to signs of the end times—(e.g., how men will feel indifferent toward God—see 2 Timothy 3:4), political unrest, a new world order involving an Antichrist (see 2 Thessalonians 2:4), severe poverty, starvation, plagues, and many diseases that will wipe out a large population of mankind (see Matthew 24:7), and changes in the weather (see

Luke 21:11, 25). There isn't anything that will occur that God hasn't already warned us about in his Word, the Bible.

My main goal in writing this book is to focus on revealing the meaning of Antichrist. Who is he? Will we be here on earth during the tribulation? Will God provide for and protect us during the tribulation? And lastly, what is meant by "the elect"?

Revelation—To Reveal

Many ministers will not go into the book of Revelation to preach the word because they believe it does not pertain to us today. It is for the ones "left behind." We will talk more about this later.

The books of Daniel and Revelation are an overlay of one another, and they reveal "end-time prophecy."

The title *Revelation* is related to the verb *reveal*. Revelation speaks of Babylon—the great whore. The word Babylon is the source of our word *babble*, meaning "confusion." There are so many confused lines of teaching among the churches today, it is a wonder any Christian can discern what is truth. The parishioners sit week after week, year after year, nodding their heads and believing every word of what their pastor is preaching in their particular denomination—never really checking him (the pastor) out in the Word of God.

Hirelings

Maybe he is a "hireling." The Bible speaks about hirelings (see John 10:12–13): "but he that is an hireling, and not the shepherd, whose own sheep are not, seeth the wolf coming, and leaveth the sheep, and fleeth: and the wolf catcheth them, and scattereth the sheep. The hireling fleeth, because he is an hireling, and careth not for the sheep."

You have a right to check out what your pastor is telling you in the Word of God without feeling like a heretic. Are we to cause problems in the church? No! If your pastor is not preaching God's Word, just excuse yourself and find a pastor who does.

Visions

Be careful about visions; anyone can have a "jalapeño nightmare."

Visions reporting how another person has been touched by God and gives revelation of future events are exciting ways in which we like to learn about truth. They proclaim to have been anointed by God and possibly are, but if their message does not align with the Word of God, precept upon precept, then I might question their authority.

People would rather read a good story, with a few scriptures thrown in here and there to show their credibility, than get their Bible out and study the Word of God. We have all become lazy and hung up on sensationalism!

We have to be so careful in what we read, because it seems that people's experience becomes gospel, whether it is checked out in God's Word or not, and we know that God's Word is the ultimate authority.

Many denominations have a milquetoast doctrine about the Word of God with little or no solid teaching. I believe that ministers are afraid to teach about hell, Satan, and end-times prophecy because it is too frightening and confusing for the congregation. Christians in the western hemisphere are materialistic and flabby (weak and lacking force), and most church denominations believe we won't be on the earth anyway; they believe we will be "snatched away." This concept is dangerous and will lead many astray! I will talk about this more later.

Many Christians, in the world of christendom, are anxiously awaiting the return of Jesus Christ who has promised to return for his church. Christians sing praises, read books, and talk continuously of his imminent return, knowing that his return could happen at any moment—or so they think. This is the "any minute" doctrine. Paul speaks of this, and I will cover this point a little further on.

I'm concerned there is not enough time to waste trying to convince people who have firmly made up their minds that their faith will not be tested in any way in the "end times." if you fall into this category and stand fully convicted on how Christ will return, then this book is not for you. But if you have an open mind about going through Scripture and getting into the meat of the Word instead of a diet of milk then I have something to share with you.

Roles Satan Plays

First of all, let's get a better look at Satan's persona. We know all the words that describe the "evil one" (e.g., liar, thief, murderer, deceiver, etc). But have you ever given much thought to the other roles he plays? He shows himself as an "angel of light" (see 2 Corinthians 11:14), "Lucifer," "Man of Sin," "Abaddon," and "Apollyon" (see Revelation 9:11), and with these few scriptures I want to set the stage for his coming role.

If you know anything about the Bible and the great controversy between Christ and Satan, then you know a great deal already about who Satan is and why he is allowed to have such a delusive influence over the world at the end of the age. Many scriptures will substantiate what Satan's role will be in the end times.

In Genesis Satan played the role of the "serpent" in the garden. In heaven Satan's name was Lucifer, the "cherub who covers" the mercy seat (Ezekiel 28:14, NKJV). Satan was the "tempter" of Christ (Matthew 4:3–9). Satan is "the man of sin" (2 Thessalonians 2:3). Satan is an "angel of light" (2 Corinthians 11:14). The number corresponding to Satan's name is "six hundred threescore and six," or 666 (Revelation 13:18).

Satan Covers the Mercy Seat

First of all let's go to the main reason that Satan lost his place in heaven as the covering cherub of the mercy seat. God had created him perfect in every way. He was beautiful (see Ezekiel 28:13), but he became prideful and jealous and wanted to have a higher position. He wanted to become God (see Ezekiel 28:14–17). Satan said, "I am God; I sit in the seat of God" (see Ezekiel 28:2).

And there was a great war in heaven. He drew a third of the angels with him as he fell to this earth (see Revelation 12:3–4).

Satan in the Garden

His first role to play was that of the serpent in the garden of Eden. He didn't appear to Eve as evil or grotesque in any way. In fact, he appeared to be knowledgeable and wise (see Ezekiel 28:3). Regarding his wisdom, Eve was beguiled by Satan (see Genesis 3:13). Otherwise, she would have been repulsed or frightened by him. Remember that Satan can appear to be anything he wishes. Satan is the great deceiver!

Satan Tempts Christ

We now have Satan tempting Christ in the wilderness (see Matthew 4:3–9). He wanted Christ to turn the stones into bread, he asked Christ to throw himself off the pinnacle of the temple, and then he took Christ to an exceedingly high mountain and showed him all the kingdoms of the world and said, "All these things I will give thee if thou wilt fall down and worship me." Satan is not only tempting the Lord God, but here we see Satan wanting to be worshipped as God. The desire to be God was what got him kicked out of heaven in the first place, and it is still Satan's obsession today.

Man of Sin

When Paul was writing to the church in Thessalonica, he was telling them about the coming of Christ (1 Thessalonians 4:16–17) and how to conduct themselves (see 1 Thessalonians 5:1–25). But the Thessalonian Christians thought Christ's return would be in their generation. They were experiencing many trials (see 2 Thessalonians 1:4–5), and they were concerned that they had missed the second coming. Paul explicitly explains to them (2 Thessalonians 2:1–4) that they should not be troubled in mind or spirit or by any letter written by him if it says that the Day of Christ is at hand. He continues in verses 3–4: "Let no man deceive you … for that day [the second coming] shall not come, except there come a falling away first, and that man of sin be revealed, the son of perdition [these names refer to SATAN]: who opposeth and exalteth himself above all that is called God … so that he as God sitteth in the temple of God, shewing himself that he is God."

Antichrist

Let's take a look at the word *Antichrist*. Go to your *Strong's Concordance*, and look up the word *anti* (*Strong's* Greek #473). It means "instead of or substitution." Look up the word *Antichrist* (*Strong's* Greek #500): an opponent of the Messiah. Look up *epithet* (Greek #5547), as in the phrase "an epithet of Jesus Christ" (e.g., Satan appearing to be the anointed one, Jesus). *Epithet* means to put on or an addition to a title (e.g., "Christ/the Anointed" or "America/the beautiful"), and here in the Greek #5547, it is Satan putting on the anointing of the Christ. He will look like Christ, but he will be "Satan/false Christ." Here is the quote from *Strong's Concordance of the Bible*, by James Strong, STD, LLD, in the Greek #5547[1]: "Christos, khris-tos'; from 5548; anointed, i.e. the Messiah, an epithet of Jesus;–Christ." The Greek numbers 5547, 5571, 5578, and 5580 are all tied together. In the *Strong's*, Greek #5578 tells us of whom they are talking about: a spurious, or false, prophet (i.e., a religious imposter). The *Strong's* Greek #5571 means liar, wicked, and deceitful. The *Strong's* Greek #5580 refers to a spurious Messiah—a pseudo, or false, Christ!

False Christ

We all know that the Antichrist is against Christ, but we now understand the meaning more in depth when it is broken down into the Greek; we see that it means or becomes something else. Anti means "instead of"; hence Antichrist means "instead of Christ" or "imposter." The word is often used in composition to denote contrast (e.g., an imposter playing the part of Jesus Christ)!

---

1   James Strong, STD, LLD, *Strong's Concordance of the Bible* (Peabody, MA: Hendrickson Publishers, 1994), 78.

Satan's Desire

Think back now to what has always been Satan's plan. He wants to be worshipped (see 2 Thessalonians 2:4). This is what Satan is determined to do, and he will let none other but himself play the role of Christ returning for the church. Remember, Satan is supernatural and will have the world worshipping him, and he will bring the nations together in a troubled time while performing miracles in the sight of men—bringing fire down from heaven (see Revelation 13:13) while doing many things that only a supernatural being could accomplish. This will not be an earthly man pretending to be Christ. Remember, the word *Antichrist* means "instead of Christ" or "in place of Christ."

The Beast and His Mark, 666

This excerpt is taken from supplementary material found in the King James Version of the Bible, published by the World Publishing Co., New York City, 1913. It states,

> The seer of Revelation appears to have had his visions in the form of a series of scenes, as in a panorama. Almost at the close (Rev. 14:9) he saw the beast you refer to. It is evidently identical with the beast described by Daniel 7:7. It is representative of the power which is said to have throughout the world's history opposed God. It appears in John's narrative in a series of forms, and is sometimes identified with a persecuting church, and sometimes is the civil power. At the culmination of its career, John saw it as the great Antichrist, who is yet to arise, who would attain to such power in the world that he would exclude many from office and from even engaging in trade, who did not acknowledge him. Only

those who bear the mark of the beast can buy or sell in that time. This mark may be a badge to be worn on forehead or hand, or as some scholars think, merely the coins to be used in business, which will bear Antichrist's title symbolized by the number 666.

I believe the mark will be more subliminal than a badge or tattoo in their foreheads. What Christians, in their right mind, would worship an Antichrist or have "666" stamped into their hand or forehead? As *Webster's Dictionary* states, *subliminal* is below the threshold of consciousness or apprehension. What is in your forehead? Your brain—and most Christians will believe this spiritual being to be the Christ and be willing to do his work, using their hands to labor for him. Christians know that 666 is the number of the Antichrist (see Revelation 13:18). We would be repulsed and I'm sure very frightened of such a diabolical being. No, this deception will take place as a very clever, insidious disguise and will be more convincing than the snake in the garden who deceived and beguiled Eve.

Even if people don't believe in Christ, or maybe they are waiting for some other religious leader to return such as the Islamic spiritual leader, the Mahdi, many people will do the bidding of Satan (posing as the Christ) because they want to continue prospering in business and proceed with life as usual. For a short time there will be prosperity and unity with peace and tranquility, but it will be only for a time. We read in Revelation 13:4 that they worship the Dragon (Satan), who has given power to the beast, saying, "Who is able to make war with him?" It's all peace, peace—not war, until he has mesmerized everyone he can and has them in his control.

Let's talk about how Satan subliminally deceives those on earth. We have learned that Satan has supernatural powers and can work miracles and "deceive the very elect" if possible (see Matthew 24:24). We read in Revelation 9:3–6, 10–11 how he does this. He is compared to the tail of a scorpion which strikes and stuns its prey. (*Webster's Dictionary* says that *stun* means "to daze, stupefy, overpower or bewilder.") How does Satan stun his prey? By his miraculous healings and by a show of love and great concern for mankind. The ones who receive his love are those who do not have the seal of God in their foreheads:

> And they [Satan's angels who fell with him] had tails like unto scorpions, and there were stings in their tails: and their power was to hurt men five months. And they had a king over them, which is the angel of the bottomless pit, whose name in the Hebrew tongue is Abaddon, but in the Greek tongue hath his name Apollyon. (Revelation 9:10–11)

These are Satan's names in the Hebrew and Greek. Satan is portraying a king—our Lord returned. The world doesn't realize how they are being hurt. They are not hurt physically (as in bodily pain), but spiritually.

In the meantime, what are the ones doing who did not take the mark of the beast? They are not living the "good life" like the rest of the world thinks they are doing. They cannot work, buy, sell, or trade, and I am afraid that many will give in and worship the false Christ because of their lack of conveniences. "Many be called, but few chosen" (see Matthew 20:16).

The false one will be incredibly convincing! Remember, he has supernatural powers, the like of which the world has never seen— but God will provide for and protect the Christians who do not take on the mark and worship the false Christ! How God does this we do not know, but do you believe God can protect you somewhere on earth while all this is going on? I do! This is where you exercise your faith in God. He is the same God yesterday, today, and tomorrow. I will say it again and again: what God did in the Old Testament He is still capable and willing to do in the New. Remember, in the Old

Testament God fed the children of Israel manna. Will he do it again? Why not!

The question arises: what about the old, the sick, and women with small children? They will need medicine and medical care! What is going to happen to these people? Don't you think God knows and understands all these things? I'm sure many will be taken to their home in heaven, in death, long before all this happens. I also believe if God wants to use these people, they will be healed and will accomplish whatever part they are to play at this crucial time.

Satan is a deceiver and a liar and plans on playing the part of our sweet and loving Jesus by sitting on the throne pretending to be God—just as Paul spoke about in 2 Thessalonians 2:2–9. Read these verses carefully:

> Be not soon shaken in mind, or be troubled, neither by spirit, nor by word, nor by letter as from us, as that the day of Christ is at hand. Let no man deceive you by any means: for that day shall not come, except there come a falling away first, and that man of sin be revealed, the son of perdition; who opposeth and exalteth himself above all that is called God, or that is worshipped; so that he as God sitteth in the temple of God, shewing himself that he is God. Remember ye not, that, when I was yet with you, I told you these things? And now ye know what withholdeth that he might be revealed in his time. (verses 2–6)

Paul was here reminding them that Satan has a specific time to be revealed, and Christ will not return until this has been accomplished.

> For the mystery of iniquity doth already work: only he who now letteth [hinders, obstructs] will let, until he be taken out of the way. (verse 7)

Satan was at work then the same as he is now, but he is not manifest upon the earth at this time. At the time of the end, God takes away the restraint and allows him (Satan) to have his way.

> And then shall that Wicked be revealed, whom the Lord shall consume with the spirit of his mouth, and shall destroy with the brightness of his coming: even him, whose coming is after the working of Satan with all power and signs and lying wonders. (verses 8–9)

Who is "that Wicked"? He is the pseudo, or false, Christ, who pretends to be Jesus but is, in actuality, Satan disguised—a wolf in sheep's clothing. He goes about "as a roaring lion ... seeking whom he may devour" (see 1 Peter 5:8).

A Strong Delusion

Paul also speaks about how God will allow those who have not studied God's Word to be sent a strong delusion that they should believe a lie. What lie? This is Satan's lie that he is the Christ.

> And for this cause God shall send them strong delusion, that they should believe a lie: that they all might be damned who believed not the truth, but had pleasure in unrighteousness. (2 Thessalonians 2:11–12)

Satan Posing as Christ

I reiterate: Satan's powers will be strongly convincing! Why? Because he has supernatural powers (see 2 Corinthians 11:14). Satan will be transformed into an "angel of light." He will be able to cause fire to come down from heaven (see Revelation 13:13), heal the sick, and do many more miraculous things—just as Christ did when He was here on earth. He will bring nations together for a healing because there is going to be a time of unrest and turmoil such as the world has never known. The world will be in economic collapse, there will be severe changes in the weather, there will be rioting in the streets and plagues. Satan will come as our savior to save us from destroying ourselves and the world we live in. He will look like Jesus, act like Jesus, and convince many that he is Jesus, but he is the "pseudo Christ"; he will almost deceive the "elect" (if you know who Satan is, then you are one of the elect of God).

Again, how do we know these things—by God's Word. You must dig deep and study the Word of God. I know I am being repetitious, but this is so important that I can't repeat it enough! See *Strong's* Greek #5580: *Antichrist* means a false Christ.

A Testing

People are going to be looking for Christ to return so that all the misery on the earth can be ended: famines, earthquakes, diseases, starvation, invasions, and changes in the weather (see Matthew 24:21–27). They will be praying and begging for His return. People will desperately be awaiting His return, but there is one test we all have to pass before Christ can come back in all His majesty and glory. Christ told us when He was here that false Christs would appear before His second coming and "If they shall say unto you, Behold, he is in the desert; go not forth: Behold, he is in the secret chambers; believe it not" (Matthew 24:26). Remember, God will not tempt us—but He does test us.

I'm sure some are asking, "Why would God test us?" God wants us to know His Word. When we are given a test in high school or at a university, it tells the teacher or instructor that we are prepared: we have studied, and we are ready. As Christians, we are to prepare ourselves the way an athlete prepares for the Olympics. Be alert, like a night watchman; otherwise, we are like the foolish virgins in Matthew 25:1–12—we are not prepared to meet our Lord.

Faithful and True

Why do you think God would allow such a deception to come upon His church? It just doesn't seem logical or fair, does it? God, most of all, wants our love and obedience. He wants to know who is truly His and who is filled with His purity and integrity and obedient to His Word, no matter what the cost—life itself, if need be. Are we better than the Master Himself who laid down His life for us?

God tells us again in Matthew 24:21–24: "Then shall be great tribulation, such as was not since the beginning of the world to this time ... but for the elect's sake those days shall be shortened." God always means what He says; have faith in Him!

The Last Trumpet

Some say the tribulation will be for the 144,000 Jews left behind to evangelize the world, and at that time, the Christians will be gone with the rapture. Let me ask you: when does Christ return for His bride (the church)? We all know that He comes at the last trump (or trumpet)—the seventh, not the fifth or sixth trump. And what happens to our bodies when Christ returns for His church, at the last trump, the "seventh" one? Our bodies shall be changed as it says in 1 Corinthians 15:52. In a moment, in the twinkling of an eye, at the "last trump" we shall be changed from the mortal to the immortal!

So here is a simple test (maybe overly simplified), but if you can feel pain, you are still in a flesh body; you have not yet been changed into your spiritual body. If you are worshipping a Jesus while you are in your flesh body, then you are worshipping the wrong Jesus! Why? Because the correct or legitimate Jesus does not come until the seventh trump, and when the trumpet sounds we will simultaneously see Christ in the clouds and receive our immortal, or celestial, bodies. Therefore, if you are still in your blue jeans and T-shirt and are capable of feeling pain, you are worshipping the Antichrist (Satan), who is the "great deceiver," pretending to be the Christ! In other words, the true Christ hasn't returned yet! Again, when does Christ return? At the last trump, the seventh trump, the farthest one out! Wake up! Read, study God's Word. He doesn't want you to be deceived!

Note: the "seven last trumps" are found in Revelation, chapters 8, 9 and 11:15. These trumps are given to seven angels to sound and alert the world about certain events that will take place at the end of time. These trumps are prophetic, and most Christians do not want to hear about them because they are so terrifying. After the six trumps have sounded and accomplished what God has directed, then the seventh trump sounds, and Christ returns for His church (God's elect)—the ones who have been faithful and true to Him!

Many Christians do not believe God will allow them to go through these trumps, because they believe they could not live through them or they want to think that God would never allow them to be so inconvenienced. This time will not be easy, but God has a way of protecting His own. He is the same God that convinced Pharaoh to let His people leave Egypt, parted the Red Sea, and provided for the Israelites in the desert forty years. So why do Christians believe that God is not the same miracle worker He was in the Old Testament or that He will not again care for His own? It amazes me to see how afraid and insecure Christians are today.

I believe many Christians become confused and fearful when it says in Mark 13:9 that they shall be delivered up to the councils and beaten and brought before the rulers and kings for Christ's sake.

Also, in Matthew 24:9 it says they shall deliver you to kill you for my name's sake. Some may be killed, if God has anointed them for this specifically appointed time, but God also says in Luke 21:18 that not a hair on your head will be harmed. Why? Because God is going to use you to speak in the councils or courts; you are of no use if you are dead. (See Mark 13:11.)

The Holy Spirit Speaks through Us

Then in verse 11 of Mark 13, we are told that we will be delivered up and should take no thought beforehand what we shall speak, but the Holy Spirit will speak for us. I believe this will be one of the greatest times the world has ever known for evangelism. Also in Luke 21:15–18, God gives us a mouth of wisdom to speak truth. Again, "But there shall not an hair on your head perish" (verse 18). Of course you have read the verse just before this that says we will be betrayed by our kinfolks and friends and be put to death. (Satan is called death; see Hebrews 2:14.) There seems to be a discrepancy here, but if you realize we are brought before Satan (Antichrist) pretending to be the Christ, is he going to kill anyone? No! He will try to convince you to believe that he is the Messiah and to worship him, and I must say it will not take much convincing because of his supernatural powers. He will be worshipped like young people worship a rock star! (Note: The reason kinfolks are "betraying" or delivering their loved ones up is because they believe they are delivering them to Jesus Christ to save their souls, but of course, in reality, they are being betrayed to Satan.) Doesn't this scripture make a great deal more sense to you now?

Those who truly know who he (the false Christ) is will be repulsed by him and the Holy Spirit will speak through them to proclaim to the world who he really is. Remember, you now know who he is! How? By the Word of God that you have studied. Your lamps are filled with oil (the Word of God). You are not fooled by his lies for one moment. Think about it for a minute; Satan wants you to believe he is the Christ, so will he be lopping off anyone's head? Of course not! He will be showing nothing but love, combined with all types of miracles and healings.

Satan's evil spirits and demons have been around on this earth for centuries. They know all about you, and they will be able to tell you exactly what you and your loved ones or friends have talked about or reveal an experience that you and your loved one had that no one else would ever know about. These encounters with Satan's spirits are going to be convincing!

Persecution

In Hebrews 2:14, Satan is called death, the power of death called the devil. Satan is death (the death of the soul). Yes, you may be put into prison, but this is where Paul did some of his greatest preaching and writing. This will be a time of testing. Are you going to go along with the milquetoast Christians who really don't know who "the false Christ-Antichrist" is because they have not studied in depth the Word of God? Baby Christians (new to the Word of God) drink the "milk of the word" (see 1 Peter 2:2), but when we mature in God's grace, we dine on the "strong meat" of the Word (see Hebrews 5:14).

There are many Christians warming the benches every Sunday morning; listening to all the great (hip) Christian music or reading just enough of the Bible to make themselves feel very self-righteous ... you get the point. I am not against making a joyful noise unto the Lord with our singing, but if this is all Christians want out of their walk with God and do not want a deeper understanding of God's Word, then they are in a very dangerous position.

Our knowledge about the "pseudo Christ" or "false Christ" will not be accepted in most or maybe any of the Christian churches. We will be about as popular as a mouse on a wedding cake. The Christians who are worshipping the false messiah will think we are heretics and certainly will not be showing us any agape love.

In my opinion, the duped Christians and the non-Christians of the world will probably be the ones that will want to do us physical harm for not worshipping this "false Christ"—who they think is Jesus returned. They will blame us for every dreadful predicament the world is in because we are obviously "evil" and are causing dissension among Christians and the world in general. This group of supporters for the false Christ will be crying out for dissenters to be done away with. They will believe we should be put into prison or worse.

The King James Version (KJV) of the Bible published by the World Publishing Company, New York, 1913, gives a question-and-answer section in the back. One of the questions, on page 33, reads: "What did Paul mean by the 'revelation of the man of sin'?" The answer: "Paul evidently believed that immediately before the second coming of Christ there would be fierce temptation and persecution (II Thess. 2:3). Christ referred to the same event in Matt. 24:20–25. The man of sin is the Antichrist or pseudo Christ, who is to deceive many. He is described in Rev. 13:11–18."

Evidently, Bible scholars did some extensive research when this Bible was published back in 1913!

The Great Deceiver

We know that Satan is the great deceiver, so what if he appeared on earth in some form of space vehicle, professing to be the Christ? What a surreal experience to encounter! It sounds far out, but this is all the world can talk about today—space travel, and wondering if there is any life beyond our galaxy. Television is inundated with all types of space travel programs. It would be hard to deny a spaceship hovering overhead! The world would go wild with excitement regarding such an event, to say nothing of having a supernatural being walk out as "the Christ" returned. This is only my imagination, and I have no biblical authority to back up this statement, but I know that an overwhelming part of the world would be totally convinced!

The True Christ

Personally, I am waiting for Christ to come in the clouds in all His magnificent glory, riding "a white horse; and he that sat upon him was called Faithful and True, and in righteousness he doth judge and make war" (see Revelation 19:11). In my opinion, God is not going to allow Satan to imitate His second coming—the one described in Revelation 19 and in Matthew 24:29–30, which states: "Immediately after the tribulation of those days shall the sun be darkened, and the moon shall not give her light, and the stars shall fall from heaven, and the powers of the heavens shall be shaken: and then shall appear the sign of the Son of man in heaven: and then shall all the tribes of the earth mourn, and they shall see the Son of man coming in the clouds of heaven with power and great glory."

A Hiding Place

Our bread and water will be sure, and the Lord will have a place for us to lay our heads. Will it be comfortable and convenient? No! See Isaiah 33:15–16: "He that walketh righteously, and speaketh uprightly; he that despiseth the gain of oppressions, that shaketh his hands from holding of bribes, that stoppeth his ears from hearing of blood, and shutteth his eyes from seeing evil; he shall dwell on high: his place of defence shall be the munitions [like a base or fortification] of rocks: bread shall be given him; his waters shall be sure." Psalm 32: 7–8 describes our secure "hiding place."

What God did in the Old Testament, He will also do in the New Testament. We are God's advocates, and He will provide a "hiding place" for those who believe. Some will go to prison, and others will not. Maybe some will be killed, but we will be ready to do whatever God has asked us to do, and we will be prepared. My goodness, as I write, there are Christians being killed all over the world for their faith. Are we really any better than they?

Remember the stoning of Stephen in the Bible? (See Acts 6–7.) He wasn't afraid; he was filled with the Holy Spirit—and we will be also. He quoted Scripture and gave a most convincing and persuasive sermon, but the council stoned him anyway.

This is a great teaching time because Satan has not yet revealed his true self, and he is still working those miracles. Look how God moved the apostle Paul around to all the different places where He wanted him to write and to speak. Was it always comfortable for him? Of course not, but he did it with joy and gladness in his heart (see Philippians 2:16–17).

A Selected Generation

I believe that God is raising up a "selected generation" that will go through this time of tribulation willingly and with great joy because they have been chosen for this particular time in history.

I see young Christian men and women remaining sexually chaste before marriage. They are setting aside the lusts and desires of the flesh so they can honor God with all their hearts and minds. I believe these will have a special anointing upon them, and they will be great witnesses in the last days.

The Rapture

I know there are many Christians who believe in the rapture of the church before any type of tribulation comes; I don't know anywhere in the Bible that it talks of Christ coming secretly for His church. I know one of these verses they stand on is Matthew 24:41–42: "Then two shall be in the field; the one shall be taken and the other left. Two women shall be grinding at the mill; the one shall be taken, and the other left. Watch therefore: for ye know not what hour your Lord doth come." His coming is not in secret; this is merely giving a description of the condition of the world or people in the end times: some will know Christ and be doing His work exposing who the Antichrist really is, and the others will be taken in deception by worshipping the false Christ. The rapture of the church (God's elect) does not occur until the seventh trumpet—the last trump (see 1 Corinthians 15:52). Then Christ shall return in all His glory. Note: when I talk about the church, the elect, or the bride of Christ, I mean Christians who have not been deceived by the Antichrist.

I'm sure many post-tribulationists would like to come forward and express their beliefs about the tribulation, but they decide to take the "low road" because the pretribulationists will use about any means to attack their opposition. Dave MacPherson substantiates my opinion in The Incredible Cover-Up (Omega Publications, 2010), page 102.

The following is quoted from pages 103 and 104 of The Incredible Cover-Up:

> Corrie ten Boom also has written about the Chinese Christians and their suffering: "The Christians were told

that they didn't have to go through tribulation and we all know how it is in China." She added that all other Christians in free lands better be prepared for what is coming to them also. And in her article "The Coming Tribulation" in the November–December 1974 *Logos Journal*, she wrote that those teaching "There will be no tribulation" and "the Christians will be able to escape all this" are really "the false teachers Jesus was warning us to expect in the latter days."

In *Sodom Had No Bible*, p. 94, British evangelist Leonard Ravenhill also emphasizes that God didn't provide a rapture in 1940 for the Chinese Christians, nor for the believers in Hungary or in Russia.

Demos Shakarian, director of the Full Gospel Businessmen, says that the Holy Spirit is now being poured out on believers to prepare them for rough times ahead. And Richard Wurmbrand told me that believers in Russia describe their existence these days as one of great tribulation and suffering. He added that America and other Western countries will have the same thing one of these days. Larry Norman's song "Right Here in America" also warns of persecution heading our way.

I have given you highlights on *The Incredible Cover-Up*, but I am not exposing the entirety of how the "rapture theory" was started; he does this with much detail and documentation. I would do him a disservice by quoting only selected passages here and there, so I suggest buying the book.

For those who do not know what *post-* and *pretribulation* mean: The pretribulationist position holds that the church will be "raptured" or "snatched out" of the world before the tribulation spoken of in Revelation begins. Post-tribulationism teaches that the church (the elect) will remain on earth while the tribulation is going on. They will be Jewish and Gentile warriors for Christ and will be equipped with the knowledge of God to stand at the end of time and expose Satan for what he really is the "Antichrist"—not our Jesus returned.

Who Are the Elect?

"*Elect* is a term variously applied. It sometimes meant the ancient church and the whole body of baptized Christians; again, it was those elected to baptism; and still again, it was the newly baptized who had just been admitted to full Christian privileges. Further, it applied to those especially chosen for the Lord's work, like His prophets and evangelists, and to those who had undergone tribulation and martyrdom. It has been applied to the whole Jewish people as chosen of God. Finally, it is applied to individuals who, not of their own merit, but through God's grace through Jesus Christ, are chosen not only to salvation, but to sanctification of the Spirit and who are holy and blameless before the Lord. They are individuals specially chosen out of the world to be heirs of salvation and witnesses for God before men. The whole subject of election has been one of acute controversy for ages and has given rise to many differences of opinion. The attitude of Christians with regard to the second coming should be one of prayer, expectancy, and constant preparation" (King James Bible, published by World Publishing Company, New York, 1913).

Since we are living in the end times, I believe we should be in constant prayer, expecting what Revelation is teaching us and become prepared for these events through God's Word. Remember, we are chosen of God for not only salvation but sanctification of the Spirit (to make productive of a spiritual blessing), and the Lord considers us blameless. Note: Are we perfect people in the flesh? Of course not, but we pray daily for forgiveness of sins and are renewed in the Spirit; God remembers our sins no more; therefore we are blameless before the Lord.

Most Christians believe the "elect" are *only* the twelve tribes of Israel (the 144,000) who are selected to go through the tribulation. The other Christians (church of Gentiles) will be gone with the rapture.

Before 1830 *church* and *elect* were mostly synonymous, while after 1830 the concepts of church and the elect split. Today most teach that the *church* means those who will be raptured, and the *elect* are only the 144,000 Jews left on earth to evangelize the world during the tribulation.

In 1830 a very sick girl by the name of Margaret MacDonald had a vision of how the church would not be here during the tribulation; two preachers later took her message as their own and proclaimed it to the world.

As noted previously, our beloved Corrie ten Boom went through the Nazi concentration camps, and there was no rapture from tribulation for these people. What makes modern-day Christians think they are so much better than those who were persecuted in the Nazi camps?

People may think, *Why should I care? What is wrong with believing in a rapture?* Because it is incorrect and offensive to God to give Christians such false hope and basically diminishing their interest in studying God's Word about what will be happening at the "end of time." Why do I believe that God is offended at those who believe in a rapture? As a parent (and God is our Father) wouldn't you be offended if you had written a love letter to your children warning them of specific events that were coming and how they would be in danger if they didn't take heed—and then instead, your children decided to listen to their friends with an exciting alternative to the disaster that you (as a parent) knew would transpire?

The real disaster is being in ignorance of who the Antichrist is and how people will be deceived into believing he is Christ returned. God is our Father, and the love letter is His Word, giving every detail we need to know of how this horrific event will occur. If they haven't read in Revelation who the Antichrist is and how he impersonates the true Christ, they are going to be caught with their knickers down. If they feel frightened now, how will they feel when all these calamities begin to take place and they are still here on earth? They will think they have been forsaken by God—that they didn't make the "cut" because they were not raptured!

What a horrible feeling! I think feeling as though you were "left behind" would be worse than realizing (early on) that you will be here on earth during this horrible time and your destiny is to be a great witness against the false Christ. At least you are going to be mentally prepared! God loves you and He will put His loving arms around you and protect you while you are doing His work. God isn't angry at those who stand against the Antichrist. "If God be for us, who can be against us?" (Romans 8:31).

God is not going to spoon-feed us! If people want to believe in something badly enough (e.g., the rapture), God will allow them enough Scripture to be convinced, and there is an abundance of "Scripture lawyers" of the Bible (preachers) who will teach intellectually (through Scripture), convincing multitudes that the church will be gone during the tribulation in the "end times."

Note: Have I been convincing enough about who the elect are, whether we will be here on earth during the tribulation, and who is the Antichrist? Probably not to most pretribulationists, but my goal in writing this book is to try to present enough information that it will tweak your interest or curiosity and you will want to begin a study of your own, if only to prove me wrong! If I have accomplished this, in my eyes, I have succeeded.

Time of Testing Shortened

This time of testing for Christians will be shortened as it says in Mark 13:20: "And except that the Lord had shortened those days, no flesh should be saved: but for the elect's sake, whom he hath chosen, he hath shortened the days." This is true; for the Christians who know who the "false messiah" is and have done their part to expose Satan for who he really is, there is no longer any need to suffer. God is not angry at the ones who stood against the Antichrist, so why should they be included in the "wrath of God" described in Revelation 16:1–17, the seven last plagues? They won't, because God's protection will be upon those who have not worshipped the "false Christ" and have the "seal of God" in their foreheads, but for those Christians who have worshipped Satan as Christ, this will be a different situation. They will suffer the seven last plagues, the "wrath of God" as mentioned in Revelation 16:1–17, and these deceived Christians will be persecuted.

The Mask Is Off

Satan has now taken off the "mask of Christ" and begins to curse the true and living God. See 2 Thessalonians 2:4, talking about the "man of sin" here (one of Satan's names) who "opposeth and exalteth himself above all that is called God, or that is worshipped; so that he, as God, sitteth in the temple of God showing himself to be God." Also in Revelation 13:5–6: "And there was given unto him [the dragon, Satan] a mouth speaking great things and blasphemies; and power was given unto him to continue forty and two months. And he opened his mouth in blasphemy against God, to blaspheme his name, and his tabernacle, and them that dwell in heaven." He is no longer pretending here to be anyone other than who he is; and he has deceived all the nations and most Christians. He has them all in his control and is now being worshipped as God, just like he has always desired and planned!

Can you imagine how these Christians will feel? They have been totally taken in by Satan, thinking he is their sweet Jesus, for whom they have been waiting. They wonder, How could this be possible? We have loved Jesus and were awaiting His rapture! These were the ones that went to church for all the wrong reasons: they wanted to be well respected in the community, they were puffed up with their preaching and teaching. Feeling sanctimonious, they went for the music and fellowship of their friends, but they neglected the most important thing: the study of God's Word in depth.

In 2 Timothy 4:3–4, we read, "For the time will come when they will not endure sound doctrine; but after their own lust shall they heap to themselves teachers, having itching ears. And they shall turn away their ears from the truth, and shall be turned unto fables." What does Christ say to these Christians at the time of His return to receive His bride? "I know you not!" God does not want those around him who have worshipped Satan, even if it is in error on their part, because in His Word, God has left every one of us everything we need to know about how His second coming will occur—not in some "fancy Dan's" best seller.

The Ten Virgins

This is one of the greatest parables I know about the condition of the church and the return of Christ: let's read about the story of the ten virgins (Matthew 25:1–12):

> 1. Then shall the kingdom of heaven be likened unto ten virgins, which took their lamps, and went forth to meet the bridegroom.

2. And five of them were wise, and five were foolish.

3. They that were foolish took their lamps, and took no oil with them:

4. but the wise took oil in their vessels with their lamps.

5. While the bridegroom tarried, they all slumbered and slept.

6. And at midnight there was a cry made, Behold, the bridegroom cometh; go ye out to meet him.

7. Then all those virgins arose, and trimmed their lamps.

8. And the foolish said unto the wise, Give us of your oil; for our lamps are gone out.

9. But the wise answered, saying, Not so; lest there be not enough for us and you: but go ye rather to them that sell, and buy for yourselves.

10. And while they went to buy, the bridegroom came; and they that were ready went in with him to the marriage: and the door was shut.

11. Afterward came also the other virgins, saying, Lord, Lord, open to us.

12. But he answered and said, Verily I say unto you, I know you not.

Note: The parable of the ten virgins is likened to the return of Christ. The "bridegroom" or the Son of God is returning for His church "the bride," at "the second coming." The "ten virgins" are the bride awaiting their bridegroom. Five of the virgins "had it together," so to speak, or were prepared for His coming. The other five virgins were foolish. They went about their lives "willy-nilly" and were not prepared spiritually for their bridegroom's return. They did not have enough oil in their lamps (spiritual knowledge) to make it to the end. They went to buy more oil, and in the meantime the bridegroom came and the only virgins that entered were the five that were spiritually prepared. The five foolish virgins were "left out in the cold," figuratively speaking. The Son of God (Jesus) is coming for His bride the church, and if she has departed and married another Jesus (the false Jesus), will the bridegroom want His bride after she has married another? No, she is no longer a virgin.

Our Lord and Savior, Jesus Christ, does not want those around Him who have their wedding garments soiled by having been married to the wrong Christ. They have made themselves adulterers! No wonder, when the true Christ comes in all His majesty and glory, they fall down and cry for the rocks to fall upon them (see Revelation 6:16). What shame they are going to feel!

In paralleling the ten virgins and how this parable relates to Christians today, those who are wise will have their lamps trimmed and ready to meet the bridegroom. They have known possibly since childhood, that there was a deeper meaning to God's Word than what they had been taught, and their souls would not stop thirsting after the living water until their lamps (souls) were filled (see Psalm 42:1–2).

There will always be the foolish and disobedient Christians who will not learn. They have their eyes and ears closed and are afraid of discernment, but take heart. As we get closer to the "end of time" things will become clearer and be better understood. It will be like a very old photograph that has been blurred over the years so that one can barely make out the images, but with modern technology (in this case, wisdom through the Holy Spirit), the photograph becomes clear and alive with color.

Blessed are those who have "eyes to see" and "ears to hear"! We have studied God's Word with the faith of a little child—filled with excitement and passion for God's Word, while not being steeped in tradition. Rejoice, because we will not be deceived by a false messiah!

In order for any of this material to make sense or have any meaning in your life, you first must accept Jesus Christ as your Savior. If you have not accepted Him, I will invite you right now to ask Christ into your life. There is a prayer format you may follow on the next page. Accepting Christ is essential or you will never understand God's Word—you must be filled with God's Spirit, the Holy Spirit.

If you are a Spirit-filled Christian, I will ask you to pray sincerely about what you have read and check me out in the Scriptures. If you are a rapture-believing Christian, I pray God has convinced you otherwise. If this information does not seem right to you now, my prayer is that you will keep it in mind, and when these things begin to occur, you will remember what you have read.

Come to Christ

If you are reading this book and you have never received Jesus Christ as your Savior, I want to ask you if you will put your trust in all that Christ has done for you, as the Son of God, and ask Him to save you right now. Just tell Him that you are sorry for all you have done wrong and believe that Christ took your sins upon Himself, taking the blame, and that He died for you. Accept Him now as your Savior!

The Shepherd's Voice

In John 10:3–5 we read: "To him the porter openeth; and the sheep hear his voice: and he calleth his own sheep by name, and leadeth them out. And when he putteth forth his own sheep, he goeth before them, and the sheep follow him: for they know his voice. And a stranger will they not follow, but will flee from him: for they know not the voice of strangers." What beautiful and comforting verses we have just read.

Summary of Signs of the End Times

Point #1: As I began to write this book, I asked, "Are we living in the 'end times'?" I spoke about Jesus's admonishment, "When ye shall see Jerusalem compassed with armies, then know that the desolation thereof is nigh" (Luke 21:20). We learned more about the desolation and saw who the desolator will be—the Antichrist or false Christ—and that he will be setting up his place of authority in the temple in Jerusalem. Of course the world believes (along with most Jewish people) that he is the Christ, but he is instead a false messiah. God allows the armies surrounding Jerusalem to destroy and take captive the non-believing Jews who have worshipped the Antichrist; the false Christ, or Satan, is removed from the temple because Christ will be setting up His kingdom in its place. (See Zechariah 14:2–4.)

Note: Many feel the Christian Jews, who have not worshipped the false Christ, will be protected in a place known as Petra. Where the Christians in America or the Western hemisphere will be protected we do not know, but it will be revealed at the proper time. We are assured of this in Isaiah 33:15–16. The twelve anointed tribes of Israel (144,000) and the "two witnesses" as mentioned in Revelation 11:3 will be evangelizing not only Jewish people in Jerusalem who have been deceived by the false Christ, but they will be evangelizing the rest of the world also. The television will be a great asset to all of these happenings; they will certainly be newsworthy!

Christ spoke in Matthew, regarding the end of the world, that this generation (meaning the "end time" generation) would not pass away before His second coming. A generation lasts some seventy to eighty years, and if we add this to 1948 when the Jews were established as a nation, we know the time is very near.

Point #2: The human and animal DNA mixing gives us a heads-up as to what the condition of the world is in—they will be lovers of self rather than lovers of God. Man wants to become like God—creating life!

Point #3: Be watchful! There is a spiritual leader of great importance among the Islamic people. His name is the Mahdi, and it is their belief that the Mahdi and Jesus Christ will be combining their efforts to unite the world under a one-world religion and government. I am not familiar with the Islamic belief, but if this is true, it will bring us right into the beginning of the tribulation. This could be another benchmark for Christians and end-times prophecy. If we see the Mahdi return as the Islamic leaders predict, how exciting this will be!

I also stated that my main goal was to focus on revealing the Antichrist and dealing with several key questions: Will we be here during the tribulation? Will God protect us during the tribulation? Who are the elect?

Revealing the Antichrist

We learned that *anti* in *Strong's Concordance* (Greek #473) means "instead of" or "substitution." *Antichrist* in the Greek (#500) means "an opponent of the Messiah." In the Greek (#5578) it means a "spurious or false Messiah," hence a false Christ or a pseudo Christ.

Will We Be Here During the Tribulation?

Yes! There is no secret return of Jesus Christ! Christ will come for His church at the last trump, which we have learned is the seventh trump and is the last trump spoken of in Revelation chapter 11:15. If you would like to know more about the tribulation and how the rapture theory got started after the 1830s, then read Dave MacPherson's book *The Incredible Cover-Up*.

Will God Protect Us During the Tribulation?

Yes, God is not mad at us! He is against those Christians and others who have worshipped the false Messiah. He promises us protection by providing us a "hiding place." Do we know where this place will be for sure? No; there are speculations, but God will lead us and provide for us at the proper time (see Isaiah 33:15–16).

There are many Christians who have not been exposed to the book of Revelation and are unaware of the seven trumpets, the number 666, and the seven last plagues. They are also unaware of how Christ returns at the seventh trump, not at the fifth or sixth trump. There is not a "secret" returning of Christ for His church. The verse that says Christ will come as a thief in the night simply means: no one knows the hour of His return, because everyone would make sure to be cleaned up and ready to go if that were the case. He wants us to be ready to meet Him every day. Live your life as though He were coming tonight. In some cases it will be tonight (for those lives which have been called back to God who gave them).

I believe I have discussed previously in depth what the "seven last trumps" are and also how Satan will be impersonating Christ at the end of time. Satan will come in peacefully like the lamb of God or Christ and deceive most of the world, if possible deceiving the very elect (see Matthew 24:24). Satan cannot deceive the "elect" because they have studied God's Word and know who Satan is portraying. They haven't rested upon their spiritual laurels, waiting to be raptured.

It seems inconceivable that a loving God would allow a "tribulation," as spoken of in Matthew 24, Mark 13, and Luke 21, to take place. Why would God allow such horrifying things to happen? People won't listen! When things are going great, they put God aside and start turning away into idolatry. What a slap in the face to God! The Israelites did this continuously throughout the Old Testament, and they were punished for it. Only when God allowed them to be captured and persecuted by heathen nations did they cry out for God to help them. It's the same way today; nothing really changes!

God does love us, but He is a jealous God (see Exodus 34:13–17) and wants us to only love Him, not a false god who will try and take His place. We are being tested—whom will we serve? It's up to you! (Note: idolatry can mean living a totally materialistic life apart from God or worshipping other false gods.)

Who Are the Elect?

The subject of the "elect" has always been of great controversy, but I think we can all agree that the elect are chosen of God—not because they are the prettiest, but because they are obedient to Him and love His word. If we are alive at the "end of time" and know who the Antichrist is, then we are part of the elect. Today, there is an abundance of books and movies depicting how Christians will disappear from earth before the tribulation occurs, but we have learned that no one leaves this earth until the seventh trumpet has sounded and Christ returns for His church.

If people look long and hard enough, there will always be a theory or someone's vision that will captivate them into believing something contrary to God's Word. In this case, Christians are looking for an escape or "rapture" so that they will not have to go through the tribulation and be inconvenienced in any way. Not only will Christians be inconvenienced, they will endure great hardships, but God promises us that He will never leave us or forsake us (see Hebrews 13:5). God will have a place of protection provided for us (see Isaiah 33:15–16), and it will be revealed when we need it most!

If rapture believers are frightened to go through the tribulation and believe they are not part of the elect, they will be the first ones deceived by the Antichrist posing as Jesus Christ. The false Christ comes in "peacefully" like the "Lamb of God" (see Revelation 13:4), not demonically, and he will convince them that he is "Jesus, the Christ," returning for his church, and he is here to "save" those who do not believe in him. He then promises he will "rapture out" his believers before any tribulation begins. If they do not know who this "Christ" is, they will fall for it like a duck takes to water!

Remember, if you know who the Antichrist is and what role he will be playing at the "end of time," you are part of the elect!

Don't be afraid of a spiritual leader posing as Christ. Satan or the Antichrist has already been defeated by Jesus Christ on the cross two thousand years ago! As Christians, all we have to do is trust in God and obey His Word! Be spiritually alert and not biblically illiterate.

About the Author

I am now in my seventies and coming to the end of my life on this earth. As I was growing up, my life was filled with much foolishness. Even though as a young child I had accepted the Lord as my Savior, there were many times that I didn't hearken unto the Word of God, but I always knew God's Spirit was with me. I have had many close calls when my life could have been snuffed out in a second, but God has always been there protecting me and watching over my family.

I live with my husband and family in the Birmingham area, and I am a member of a God-fearing church. I will not mention the name of the church because I could possibly cause dissension among its leaders regarding this message—and this is not my reason for writing this book. There will come a day when I will step forward in person, if I am still alive, and stand against the "false messiah," the "evil one," but today is not the day.

I really didn't want to write something so controversial! As humans, we always want something to be done, but we want someone else to do it. This time it is my turn to be that someone else—especially since my encounter with Larry at the Christian bookstore.

My persistence in writing this book was not of my own accord, but by the encouragement of the Holy Spirit. He gave me confidence each day to keep on going, letting me know, in a way that only God can, "You can do it, but only in My strength."

What I have written is for the future, or basically "uncharted" material, but in my reasoning, God's "warnings" in the Bible are written like a map for us to see (like you would chart a road map), so I'm not sure if it will fit into the uncharted category or not—you will have to make that decision yourself.

I love the Lord with all my heart, and I know what happens to those who mislead God's children. I am not a teacher or preacher of God's Word—only someone who wants people to dig deeper into the Word of God and let the Holy Spirit guide them.

My beliefs in the Bible are very conservative. I believe in the virgin birth. I believe Christ and Christ alone is my salvation (nothing I can do), and I believe God is in three persons, as one. I do not believe in abortion or in universalism. Straight and narrow is the gateway to heaven, and broad is the way which leadeth to destruction. (See Matthew 7:13–14.)

On the following pages are some of my favorite Psalms. I'm sure you have read many of them also. These verses are powerful old favorites and give great comfort to those who rely on God's help in the time of need.

In His hands,

MARY E. PRESTON

Favorite Psalms That Comfort Me

Psalm 91:4

He shall cover thee with his feathers, and under his wings shalt thou trust: his truth shall be thy shield and buckler.

(This Psalm alone kept me going.)

Psalm 3

1. LORD, how are they increased that trouble me! many are they that rise up against me.

2. Many there be which say of my soul, There is no help for him in God. Selah.

3. But thou, O LORD, art a shield for me; my glory, and the lifter up of mine head.

4. I cried unto the LORD with my voice, and he heard me out of his holy hill. Selah.

5. I laid me down and slept; I awaked; for the LORD sustained me.

6. I will not be afraid of ten thousands of people, that have set themselves against me round about.

7. Arise, O LORD; save me, O my God: for thou hast smitten all mine enemies upon the cheek bone; thou hast broken the teeth of the ungodly.

8. Salvation belongeth unto the LORD; thy blessing is upon thy people. Selah.

Psalm 8

1. O LORD, our Lord, how excellent is thy name in all the earth! who hast set thy glory above the heavens.

2. Out of the mouth of babes and sucklings hast thou ordained strength because of thine enemies, that thou mightest still the enemy and the avenger.

3. When I consider thy heavens, the work of thy fingers, the moon and the stars, which thou hast ordained;

4. what is man, that thou art mindful of him? and the son of man, that thou visitest him?

5. For thou hast made him a little lower than the angels, and hast crowned him with glory and honour.

6. Thou madest him to have dominion over the works of thy hands; thou hast put all things under his feet:

7. all sheep and oxen, yea, and the beasts of the field;

8. the fowl of the air, and the fish of the sea, and whatsoever passeth through the paths of the seas.

9. O LORD our Lord, how excellent is thy name in all the earth!

Psalm 15

1. LORD, who shall abide in thy tabernacle? who shall dwell in thy holy hill?

2. He that walketh uprightly, and worketh righteousness, and speaketh the truth in his heart.

3. He that backbiteth not with his tongue, nor doeth evil to his neighbour, nor taketh up a reproach against his neighbour.

4. In whose eyes a vile person is contemned; but he honoureth them that fear the LORD. He that sweareth to his own hurt, and changeth not.

5. He that putteth not out his money to usury, nor taketh reward against the innocent. He that doeth these things shall never be moved.

Psalm 23

1. The LORD is my shepherd; I shall not want.

2. He maketh me to lie down in green pastures: he leadeth me beside the still waters.

3. He restoreth my soul: he leadeth me in the paths of righteousness for his name's sake.

4. Yea, though I walk through the valley of the shadow of death, I will fear no evil: for thou art with me; thy rod and thy staff they comfort me.

5. Thou preparest a table before me in the presence of mine enemies: thou anointest my head with oil; my cup runneth over.

6. Surely goodness and mercy shall follow me all the days of my life: and I will dwell in the house of the LORD for ever.

Psalm 34

1. I will bless the LORD at all times: his praise shall continually be in my mouth.

2. My soul shall make her boast in the LORD: the humble shall hear thereof, and be glad.

3. O magnify the LORD with me, and let us exalt his name together.

4. I sought the LORD, and he heard me, and delivered me from all my fears.

5. They looked unto him, and were lightened: and their faces were not ashamed.

6. This poor man cried, and the LORD heard him, and saved him out of all his troubles.

7. The angel of the LORD encampeth round about them that fear him, and delivereth them.

8. O taste and see that the LORD is good: blessed is the man that trusteth in him.

9. O fear the LORD, ye his saints: for there is no want to them that fear him.

10. The young lions do lack, and suffer hunger: but they that seek the LORD shall not want any good thing.

11. Come, ye children, hearken unto me: I will teach you the fear of the LORD.

12. What man is he that desireth life, and loveth many days, that he may see good?

13. Keep thy tongue from evil, and thy lips from speaking guile.

14. Depart from evil, and do good; seek peace, and pursue it.

15. The eyes of the LORD are upon the righteous, and his ears are open unto their cry.

16. The face of the LORD is against them that do evil, to cut off the remembrance of them from the earth.

17. The righteous cry, and the LORD heareth, and delivereth them out of all their troubles.

18. The LORD is nigh unto them that are of a broken heart; and saveth such as be of a contrite spirit.

19. Many are the afflictions of the righteous: but the LORD delivereth him out of them all.

20. He keepeth all his bones: not one of them is broken.

21. Evil shall slay the wicked: and they that hate the righteous shall be desolate.

22. The LORD redeemeth the soul of his servants: and none of them that trust in him shall be desolate.

Psalm 37

1. Fret not thyself because of evildoers, neither be thou envious against the workers of iniquity.

2. For they shall soon be cut down like the grass, and wither as the green herb.

3. Trust in the LORD, and do good; so shalt thou dwell in the land, and verily thou shalt be fed.

4. Delight thyself also in the LORD: and he shall give thee the desires of thine heart.

5. Commit thy way unto the LORD; trust also in him; and he shall bring it to pass.

6. And he shall bring forth thy righteousness as the light, and thy judgment as the noonday.

7. Rest in the LORD, and wait patiently for him: fret not thyself because of

him who prospereth in his way, because of the man who bringeth wicked devices to pass.

8. Cease from anger, and forsake wrath: fret not thyself in any wise to do evil.

9. For evildoers shall be cut off: but those that wait upon the LORD, they shall inherit the earth.

10. For yet a little while, and the wicked shall not be: yea, thou shalt diligently consider his place, and it shall not be.

11. But the meek shall inherit the earth; and shall delight themselves in the abundance of peace.

12. The wicked plotteth against the just, and gnasheth upon him with his teeth.

13. The LORD shall laugh at him: for he seeth that his day is coming.

14. The wicked have drawn out the sword, and have bent their bow, to cast down the poor and needy, and to slay such as be of upright conversation.

15. Their sword shall enter into their own heart, and their bows shall be broken.

16. A little that a righteous man hath is better than the riches of many wicked.

17. For the arms of the wicked shall be broken: but the LORD upholdeth the righteous.

18. The LORD knoweth the days of the upright: and their inheritance shall be for ever.

19. They shall not be ashamed in the evil time: and in the days of famine they shall be satisfied.

20. But the wicked shall perish, and the enemies of the LORD shall be as the fat of lambs: they shall consume; into smoke shall they consume away.

21. The wicked borroweth, and payeth not again: but the righteous sheweth mercy, and giveth.

22. For such as be blessed of him shall inherit the earth; and they that be cursed of him shall be cut off.

23. The steps of a good man are ordered by the LORD: and he delighteth in his way.

24. Though he fall, he shall not be utterly cast down: for the LORD upholdeth him with his hand.

25. I have been young, and now am old; yet have I not seen the righteous forsaken, nor his seed begging bread.

26. He is ever merciful, and lendeth; and his seed is blessed.

27. Depart from evil, and do good; and dwell for evermore.

28. For the LORD loveth judgment, and forsaketh not his saints; they are preserved forever: but the seed of the wicked shall be cut off.

29. The righteous shall inherit the land, and dwell therein for ever.

30. The mouth of the righteous speaketh wisdom, and his tongue talketh of judgment.

31. The law of his God is in his heart; none of his steps shall slide.

32. The wicked watcheth the righteous, and seeketh to slay him.

33. The LORD will not leave him in his hand, nor condemn him when he is judged.

34. Wait on the LORD, and keep his way, and he shall exalt thee to inherit the land: when the wicked are cut off, thou shalt see it.

35. I have seen the wicked in great power, and spreading himself like a green bay tree.

36. Yet he passed away, and, lo, he was not: yea, I sought him, but he could not be found.

37. Mark the perfect man, and behold the upright: for the end of that man is peace.

38. But the transgressors shall be destroyed together: the end of the wicked shall be cut off.

39. But the salvation of the righteous is of the LORD: he is their strength in the time of trouble.

40. And the LORD shall help them, and deliver them: he shall deliver them from the wicked, and save them, because they trust in him.

Psalm 43

1. Judge me, O God, and plead my cause against an ungodly nation: O deliver me from the deceitful and unjust man.

2. For thou art the God of my strength: why dost thou cast me off? why go I mourning because of the oppression of the enemy?

3. O send out thy light and thy truth: let them lead me; let them bring me unto thy holy hill, and to thy tabernacles.

4. Then will I go unto the altar of God, unto God my exceeding Joy: yea, upon the harp will I praise thee, O God my God.

5. Why art thou cast down, O my soul? and why art thou disquieted within me? hope in God: for I shall yet praise him, who is the health of my countenance, and my God.

Psalm 46

1. God is our refuge and strength, a very present help in trouble.

2. Therefore will not we fear, though the earth be removed, and though the mountains be carried into the midst of the sea;

3. Though the waters thereof roar and be troubled, though the mountains shake with the swelling thereof. Selah.

4. There is a river, the streams whereof shall make glad the city of God, the holy place of the tabernacles of the most High.

5. God is in the midst of her; she shall not be moved: God shall help her, and that right early.

6. The heathen raged, the kingdoms were moved: he uttered his voice, the earth melted.

7. The LORD of hosts is with us; the God of Jacob is our refuge. Selah.

8. Come, behold the works of the LORD, what desolations he hath made in the earth.

9. He maketh wars to cease unto the end of the earth; he breaketh the bow, and cutteth the spear in sunder; he burneth the chariot in the fire.

10. Be still, and know that I am God: I will be exalted among the heathen, I will be exalted in the earth.

11. The LORD of hosts is with us; the God of Jacob is our refuge. Selah.

Psalm 56

1. Be merciful unto me, O God: for man would swallow me up; he fighting daily oppresseth me.

2. Mine enemies would daily swallow me up: for they be many that fight against me, O thou most High.

3. What time I am afraid, I will trust in thee.

4. In God I will praise his word, in God I have put my trust; I will not fear what flesh can do unto me.

5. Every day they wrest my words: all their thoughts are against me for evil.

6. They gather themselves together, they hide themselves, they mark my steps, when they wait for my soul.

7. Shall they escape by iniquity? in thine anger cast down the people, O God.

8. Thou tellest my wanderings: put thou my tears into thy bottle: are they not in thy book?

9. When I cry unto thee, then shall mine enemies turn back: this I know; for God is for me.

10. In God will I praise his word: in the LORD will I praise his word.

11. In God have I put my trust: I will not be afraid what man can do unto me.

12. Thy vows are upon me, O God: I will render praises unto thee.

13. For thou hast delivered my soul from death: wilt not thou deliver my feet from falling, that I may walk before God in the light of the living?

Psalm 61

1. Hear my cry, O God; attend unto my prayer.

2. From the end of the earth will I cry unto thee, when my heart is overwhelmed: lead me to the rock that is higher than I.

3. For thou hast been a shelter for me, and a strong tower from the enemy.

4. I will abide in thy tabernacle for ever: I will trust in the covert of thy wings. Selah.

5. For thou, O God, hast heard my vows: thou hast given me the heritage of those that fear thy name.

6. Thou wilt prolong the king's life: and his years as many generations.

7. He shall abide before God for ever: O prepare mercy and truth, which may preserve him.

8. So will I sing praise unto thy name for ever, that I may daily perform my vows.

Psalm 62

1. Truly my soul waiteth upon God: from him cometh my salvation.

2. He only is my rock and my salvation; he is my defence; I shall not be greatly moved.

3. How long will ye imagine mischief against a man? Ye shall be slain all of you: as a bowing wall shall ye be, and as a tottering fence.

4. They only consult to cast him down from his excellency: they delight in lies: they bless with their mouth, but they curse inwardly. Selah.

5. My soul, wait thou only upon God; for my expectation is from him.

6. He only is my rock and my salvation: he is my defence; I shall not be moved.

7. In God is my salvation and my glory: the rock of my strength, and my refuge, is in God.

8. Trust in him at all times; ye people, pour out your heart before him: God is a refuge for us. Selah.

9. Surely men of low degree are vanity, and men of high degree are a lie: to be laid in the balance, they are altogether lighter than vanity.

10. Trust not in oppression, and become not vain in robbery: if riches increase, set not your heart upon them.

11. God hath spoken once; twice have I heard this; that power belongeth unto God.

12. Also unto thee, O Lord, belongeth mercy: for thou renderest to every man according to his work.

Psalm 63

1. O God, thou art my God; early will I seek thee: my soul thirsteth for thee, my flesh longeth for thee, my flesh longeth for thee in a dry and thirsty land, where no water is;

2. To see thy power and thy glory, so as I have seen thee in the sanctuary.

3. Because thy lovingkindness is better than life, my lips shall praise thee.

4. Thus will I bless thee while I live: I will lift up my hands in thy name.

5. My soul shall be satisfied as with marrow and fatness; and my mouth shall praise thee with joyful lips:

6. When I remember thee upon my bed, and meditate on thee in the night watches.

7. Because thou hast been my help, therefore in the shadow of thy wings will I rejoice.

8. My soul followeth hard after thee: thy right hand upholdeth me.

9. But those that seek my soul, to destroy it, shall go into the lower parts of the earth.

10. They shall fall by the sword: they shall be a portion for the foxes.

11. But the king shall rejoice in God; every one that sweareth by him shall glory: but the mouth of them that speak lies shall be stopped.

Psalm 71

1. In thee, O LORD, do I put my trust: let me never be put to confusion.

2. Deliver me in thy righteousness, and cause me to escape: incline thine ear unto me, and save me.

3. Be thou my strong habitation, whereunto I may continually resort: thou hast given commandment to save me; for thou art my rock and my fortress.

4. Deliver me, O my God, out of the hand of the wicked, out of the land of the unrighteous and cruel man.

5. For thou art my hope, O Lord GOD: thou art my trust from my youth.

6. By thee have I been holden up from the womb: thou art he that took me out of my mother's bowels: my praise shall be continually of thee.

7. I am as a wonder unto many; but thou art my strong refuge.

8. Let my mouth be filled with thy praise and with thy honour all the day.

9. Cast me not off in the time of old age; forsake me not when my strength faileth.

10. For mine enemies speak against me; and they that lay wait for my soul take counsel together,

11. Saying, God hath forsaken him: persecute and take him; for there is none to deliver him.

12. O God, be not far from me: O my God, make haste for my help.

13. Let them be confounded and consumed that are adversaries to my soul; let them be covered with reproach and dishonour that seek my hurt.

14. But I will hope continually, and will yet praise thee more and more.

15. My mouth shall shew forth thy righteousness and thy salvation all the day; for I know not the number thereof.

16. I will go in the strength of the Lord GOD: I will make mention of thy righteousness, even of thine only.

17. O God, thou hast taught me from my youth: and hitherto have I declared thy wondrous works.

18. Now also when I am old and greyheaded, O God, forsake me not; until I have shewed thy strength unto this generation, and thy power to every one that is to come.

19. Thy righteousness also, O God, is very high, who hast done great things: O God, who is like unto thee!

20. Thou, which hast shewed me great and sore troubles, shalt quicken me again, and shalt bring me up again from the depths of the earth.

21. Thou shalt increase my greatness, and comfort me on every side.

22. I will also praise thee with the psaltery, even thy truth, O my God: unto thee will I sing with the harp, O thou Holy One of Israel.

23. My lips shall greatly rejoice when I sing unto thee; and my soul, which thou hast redeemed.

24. My tongue also shall talk of thy righteousness all the day long: for they are confounded, for they are brought unto shame, that seek my hurt.

Psalm 91

1. He that dwelleth in the secret place of the most High shall abide under the shadow of the Almighty.

2. I will say of the LORD, He is my refuge and my fortress: my God; in him will I trust.

3. Surely he shall deliver thee from the snare of the fowler, and from the noisome pestilence.

4. He shall cover thee with his feathers, and under his wings shalt thou trust: his truth shall be thy shield and buckler.

5. Thou shalt not be afraid for the terror by night; nor for the arrow that flieth by day;

6. Nor for the pestilence that walketh in darkness; nor the destruction that wasteth at noonday.

7. A thousand shall fall at thy side, and ten thousand at thy right hand; but it shall not come nigh thee.

8. Only with thine eyes shalt thou behold and see the reward of the wicked.

9. Because thou hast made the LORD, which is my refuge, even the most High, thy habitation;

10. There shall no evil befall thee, neither shall any plague come nigh thy dwelling.

11. For he shall give his angels charge over thee, to keep thee in all thy ways.

12. They shall bear thee up in their hands, lest thou dash thy foot against a stone.

13. Thou shalt tread upon the lion and adder: the young lion and the dragon shalt thou trample under feet.

14. Because he hath set his love upon me, therefore will I deliver him: I will set him on high, because he hath known my name.

15. He shall call upon me, and I will answer him: I will be with him in trouble; I will deliver him, and honour him.

16. With long life will I satisfy him, and shew him my salvation.

Psalm 100

1. Make a joyful noise unto the LORD, all ye lands.

2. Serve the LORD with gladness: come before his presence with singing.

3. Know ye that the LORD he is God: it is he that hath made us, and not we ourselves; we are his people, and the sheep of his pasture.

4. Enter into his gates with thanksgiving, and into his courts with praise: be thankful unto him, and bless his name.

5. For the LORD is good; his mercy is everlasting; and his truth endureth to all generations.

Psalm 117

1. O praise the LORD, all ye nations: praise him, all ye people.

2. For his merciful kindness is great toward us: and the truth of the LORD endureth for ever. Praise ye the LORD.

Psalm 121

1. I will lift up mine eyes unto the hills, from whence cometh my help.

2. My help cometh from the LORD, which made heaven and earth.

3. He will not suffer thy foot to be moved: he that keepeth thee will not slumber.

4. Behold, he that keepeth Israel shall neither slumber nor sleep.

5. The LORD is thy keeper: the LORD is thy shade upon thy right hand.

6. The sun shall not smite thee by day, nor the moon by night.

7. The LORD shall preserve thee from all evil: he shall preserve thy soul.

8. The LORD shall preserve thy going out and thy coming in from this time forth, and even for evermore.

Psalm 123

1. Unto thee lift I up mine eyes, O thou that dwellest in the heavens.

2. Behold, as the eyes of servants look into the hand of their masters, and as the eyes of a maiden unto the hand of her mistress; so our eyes wait upon the LORD our God, until that he have mercy upon us.

3. Have mercy upon us, O LORD, have mercy upon us: for we are exceedingly filled with contempt.

4. Our soul is exceedingly filled with the scorning of those that are at ease, and with the contempt of the proud.

Psalm 131

1. Lord, my heart is not haughty, nor mine eyes lofty: neither do I exercise myself in great matters, or in things too high for me.

2. Surely I have behaved and quieted myself, as a child that is weaned of his mother: my soul is even as a weaned child.

3. Let ISRAEL hope in the LORD from henceforth and for ever.

Psalm 147

1. Praise ye the LORD: for it is good to sing praises unto our God; for it is pleasant; and praise is comely.

2. The LORD doth build up Jerusalem: he gathereth together the outcasts of Israel.

3. He healeth the broken in heart, and bindeth up their wounds.

4. He telleth the number of the stars; he calleth them all by their names.

5. Great is our Lord, and of great power: his understanding is infinite.

6. The LORD lifteth up the meek: he casteth the wicked down to the ground.

7. Sing unto the LORD with thanksgiving; sing praise upon the harp unto our God:

8. Who covereth the heaven with clouds, who prepareth rain for the earth, who maketh grass to grow upon the mountains.

9. He giveth to the beast his food, and to the young ravens which cry.

10. He delighteth not in the strength of the horse: he taketh not pleasure in the legs of a man.

11. The LORD taketh pleasure in them that fear him, in those that hope in his mercy.

12. Praise the LORD, O Jerusalem; praise thy God, O Zion.

13. For he hath strengthened the bars of thy gates; he hath blessed thy children within thee.

14. He maketh peace in the borders, and filleth thee with the finest of the wheat.

15. He sendeth forth his commandment upon earth: his word runneth very swiftly.

16. He giveth snow like wool: he scattereth the hoarfrost like ashes.

17. He casteth forth his ice like morsels: who can stand before his cold?

18. He sendeth out his word, and melteth them: he causeth his wind to blow, and the waters flow.

19. He sheweth his word unto Jacob, his statutes and his judgments unto Israel.

20. He hath not dealt so with any nation: and as for his judgments, they have not known them. Praise ye the LORD.

Psalm 150

1. Praise ye the LORD. Praise God in his sanctuary: praise him in the firmament of his power.

2. Praise him for his mighty acts: praise him according to his excellent greatness.

3. Praise him with the sound of the trumpet: praise him with the psaltery and harp.

4. Praise him with the timbrel and dance: praise him with stringed instruments and organs.

5. Praise him upon the loud cymbals: praise him upon the high sounding cymbals.

6. Let every thing that hath breath praise the LORD. Praise ye the LORD.